Fatherless Heart

Interactive Workbook

The Story of a Fatherless Child

Laurie Ford, LCMHC

Copyright NOTICE

Table of Contents

SECTION 1

ACKNOWLEDGEMENTS

DEDICATION

GOD'S CHOSEN FATHERLESS CHILD

ENCOURAGEMENT

FATHERLESS PERMISSION SLIP

Acknowledgements

When God gave me this assignment, I knew this was something bigger than I could ever imagine.

Thank you, God, for trusting me with this vision.

Thank you to my husband, Eddie Ford, Jr., my family, my therapist, Pastors, and friends who supported and encouraged me throughout this journey.

DEDICATION

This book is dedicated to the fatherless child.

- The child who has an absent father.
- The child who doesn't know their biological father.
- The child whose father is present but not active.

Through many obstacles, God has turned my scars into beauty marks. He has allowed me to endure pain as a part of my process knowing that he would never leave my side. This book required a new level of vulnerability that the world needs to hear. I've learned sharing my story is necessary to help the people assigned to my story. I understand now that I am called to the fatherless. I have been assigned to help bring clarity to your specific situation and emotions.

Allow this workbook to help you heal, release, and normalize your narrative.

God's Chosen Fatherless Author

Laurie Ford is a God-fearing woman who was chosen by God to help others during their healing process. She has accepted the call on her life and is committed to walking with you during this transition called LIFE.

The purpose of this workbook is to:

- Share Laurie's fatherless testimony with you including her experiences with her substitute father, her grandfather
- Normalize the healing process of being fatherless
- Help you work through your emotions by completing various activities
- Share her healing process

Meet The Author:

Laurie Ford

*Licensed Clinical
Mental Health Counselor*

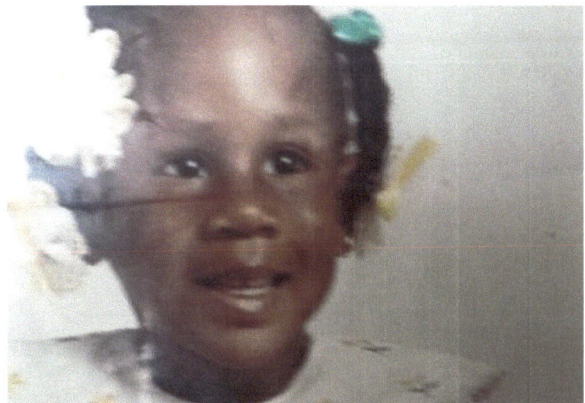

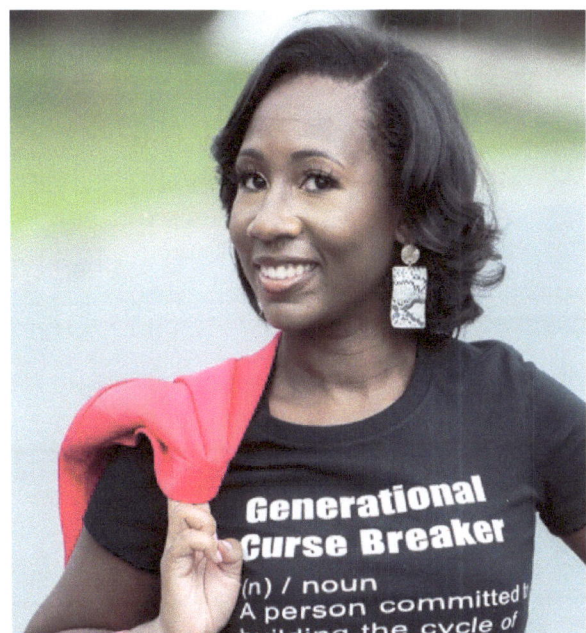

Generational Curse Breaker
(n) / noun
A person committed
building the cycle of

ENCOURAGEMENT

You are called and chosen.
The absence of your father doesn't downgrade
your value and purpose.
There is worth in a fatherless heart.
There is still love that is necessary to give.
You are called to be set apart.
Release those negative emotions.
Your father's absence "IS NOT YOUR FAULT".
Let go of the blame and guilt.
There is nothing you could have done differently
or said that could change your father's behaviors.
You are not alone.
I understand what you are going through and
God has never left your side.
God will mend your broken heart and fill every
void in your life.
Understand, your life still matters.

FATHERLESS PERMISSIONSLIP

I GIVE MYSELF PERMISSION TO.....

Instructions: In this section, give yourself permission to *feel*. All those emotions that you felt you had to suppress, let's address them now. Read each statement and repeat them aloud.

ONE — I give myself permission to grieve the absence of my father

TWO — I give myself permission to desire a relationship with a father figure

THREE — I give myself persmission to ask questions about my father

FOUR — I give myself permission to embrace the emotions I am feeling when I think about my father

FIVE — I give myself permission to accept the life that I was born into knowing I have the power to change my mindset

SIX — I give myself permission to search for my father

Signature_____   Date_____

SECTION 2

DADDY ISSUES

SAD

LETTER TO MY
UNKNOWN FATHER

LETTER FROM THE
FATHERLESS HEART

ABSENT FATHER

Daddy Issues

Daddy issues often occurs when you grow up without a father in your life. Your father could be present but not active; your father could be unknown; or, your father could be deceased.

Whatever your personal story, your emotions can be labeled as daddy issues. I realized early that I encountered daddy issues. I began looking for what I longed for from my dad in my relationships. I would attach myself to the wrong relationships searching for a dad's love, instead of friendship with my peers. I experienced heart breaks, abuse, and neglect trying to fill a void that was unfillable.

In college, I was attracted to older men who were controlling, in reality, but I viewed it as protection which was missing from the father who raised me. Being able to say the word 'daddy' is not something I take lightly.

Growing up, I never said the word 'daddy' or 'dad' and that used to bother me daily. I always knew I would've been a daddy's girl just by my thoughts and my interactions with my uncles.

I felt like the opportunity was taken away from me and that made me sad. Not knowing who my biological father was bothered me emotionally for years. Not knowing if I had a sibling was also a question. I remember seeing different black men out at stores and I would wonder if some of the men were my dad.

I remember having a conversation with a man at the flee market who stated he knew my mom. After our conversation, I thought he could've been my dad. It was tough looking around at my friends or family members experiencing a relationship I never thought was possible for me.

Daddy Issues

Imagine being surrounded by everyone else's father and not your own. Imagine not being able to identify traits and characteristics you may have with your father. The feeling was sometimes indescribable. I realized the word 'daddy' for me, would have a different meaning in my future.

SAD

You have the right to feel sad!
I realized I had the right to feel sad. The chance of knowing my father was taken away from me and I wasn't prepared for the lasting effects as a child and young adult.

Today, I want you to affirm your rights. Sometimes, when we are still going through the healing process, we cheat ourselves out of our true feelings. Today, I am giving you the right to just "FEEL".

In the section below, write down your rights to feel.
Fill in the blanks: *I have the right to FEEL...*

I have a right to feel
_____

I have a right to feel
_____

I have a right to feel
_____

I have a right to feel
_____

I have a right to feel
_____

I have a right to feel
_____

I have a right to feel
_____

I have a right to feel
_____

I have a right to feel
_____

I have a right to feel
_____

I have a right to feel
_____

I have a right to feel
_____

I have a right to feel
_____

I have a right to feel
_____

I have a right to feel
_____

LETTER TO MY UNKNOWN FATHER

Dear Unknown Father,

I know you've never met me and I'm not sure if you even care to know me. I am Laurie Ford, your daughter. I am 32 years old and I live in North Carolina. I am writing this letter to introduce myself to you and to tell you my thoughts and feelings about our non-existing relationship. As I try to wrap my head around how you look, I can't help but get emotional because I have no clue where to begin. Before my mom passed away, she told me that you never knew of my existence, but she also told me that another guy was my father. Yes, sounds suspect to me as well. As I reflect back on my childhood, I was very confused and longed for you. I would often say to myself I wonder how he looks? Do I have any siblings? I wonder if we have the same nose? I wonder if he has dark skin? I wonder if he even knows who I am?

Even as an adult, I still think about these questions. I wish I could see you and embrace your hugs. In my imagination, I would reach out to the Oprah show and she would help me find you. There are so many things I want to ask you. There are so many experiences I feel that I have missed. I wish I could have experienced a daddy/daughter dance with you. I wish you could have taught me how to ride a bike. Not being able to say the word 'Daddy' really bothered me. I watched my friends' relationships with their dads and I immediately felt abandoned. I felt abandoned for years and I struggled with so much hurt and resentment. I used to let anxiety get the best of me as a result of not knowing you. Although I am an adult now, my heart and mind still desire a connection with you. I want my children to meet their grandfather.

I have learned so much about myself over the years from this experience. I learned I struggled so much with rejection and hurt. I learned I had control issues. I used to question my worth and value based on my parents' rejection of me. I have now learned that not knowing you was a part of God's purpose for my life. God has used this fatherless heart in so many ways. I am now able to help so many others who struggle in this area. I remember sitting on the couch talking to my therapist about you. I would ask her why am I crying over a man I didn't even know? Why am I crying over a man that may not even know of my existence. She replied to me with comfort stating crying and wanting a connection with my father was normal. I have given the task of finding you to God. I have peace now whether we meet or not knowing God has covered me in this area and he is using me in this area. Until we meet or don't meet. Take care.

Your Daughter,
Laurie Ford

Now, write your own letter from your heart to your father on the following page.

11

LETTERS FROM THE FATHERLESS HEART

Dear _____,

_____
_____
_____
_____
_____
_____
_____
_____
_____
_____
_____
_____
_____
_____
_____
_____
_____
_____
_____
_____
_____
_____
_____
_____
_____
_____

ABSENT FATHER

In this section, you will create a checklist of what your father missed by being absent in your life.

Here's a list that I created for myself:

- Building a great relationship with your daughter
- My first steps
- My first words
- Purity conversations
- Teaching me how to be loved by a man
- Daddy/Daughter Dances
- Cheerleading and talent show performances
- Graduations (Middle/High/College)
- Giving me away at my wedding
- Home-buying process
- Being able to comfort me
- Being able to protect me
- Being a provider
- My extrovert personality

As a result of your absence, you missed:

_____

_____

_____

_____

_____

_____

_____

_____

_____

_____

_____

_____

_____

_____

SECTION 3

I HAD A FATHER FIGURE, BUT STILL FELT EMPTY

RAISED BY MY GRANDPARENTS

DID I MAKE YOU PROUD, GRANDPA?

I DID THE BEST I COULD

THE INVISIBLE CHILD: A POEM

Raised by my Grandparents

My grandpa raised me, but I still felt empty. It was hard growing up not knowing my biological father, but it was harder being raised by my grandpa and still feeling rejected. Most of our neighbors thought my sisters and I had the best life. Their focus was on the material things we had and the amount of family members' support. However, for me that wasn't enough. I needed the basics such as love, protection, safety, nurturing, and affection. I remember thinking, "Why would you take us from our mom if you couldn't give me the fatherly love that I needed?"

Watching my grandpa consume alcohol every weekend was very traumatic. It wasn't so much the alcohol, it was his behavior. It didn't feel good to hear my grandpa stumble in the house because he was drunk. I remember thinking as a child that if he doesn't stop drinking soon, I will lose another parent. I used to ask God, "Why me? Why do I have to witness this crazy behavior?" I wanted to just sleep and wake up and it all be a nightmare. The rest of my friends looked forward to the weekend, but I didn't. I didn't want to see Friday because I knew I had to deal with an alcoholic for three days.

My siblings and I were very protective of each other, especially when my grandpa would drink. He would come in the room and wake me up just to discipline me regarding something I did in school earlier in the week. Can you imagine being deep in your sleep and someone waking you up just to yell and discipline you with the overpowering smell of alcohol on their breath? Hard to even imagine, right?

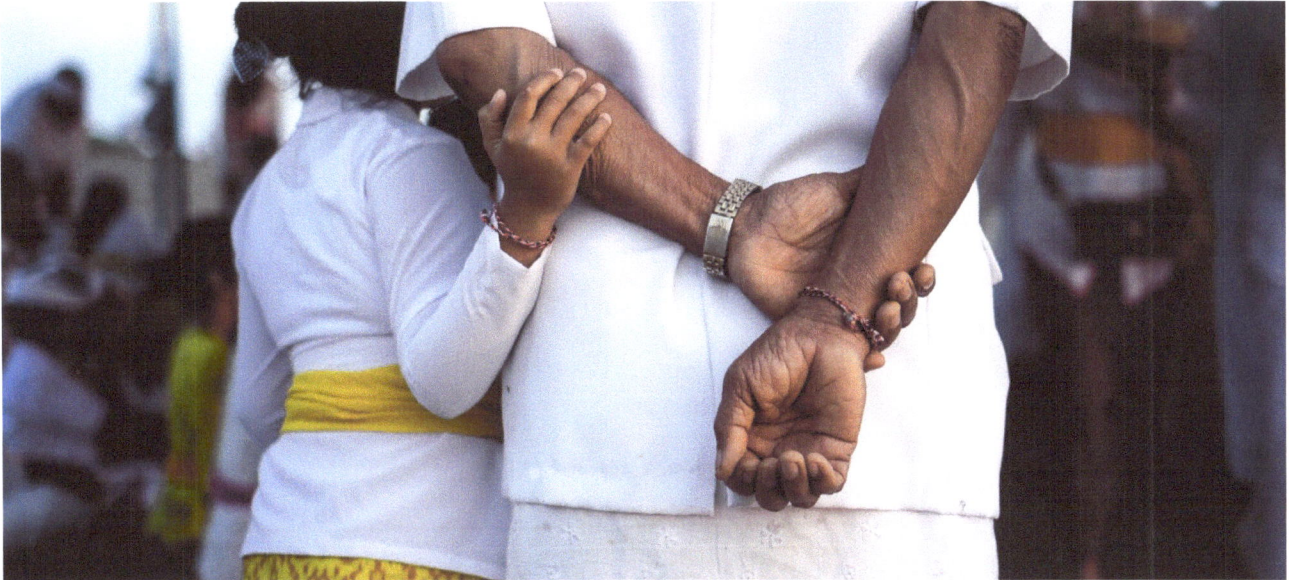

Have you ever wondered if your accomplishments matter? I used to think to myself how much do I need to accomplish to be visible to my grandpa. How many times do I need to win an award to feel noticed? How many things do I need to do in order to become the child he could say that he was proud of?

Growing up, I had a lot of siblings and I was in competition with them all based on the family dynamics in my household. I felt that in order to be noticed in my house by my grandpa, I had to be doing or accomplishing something to feel valued. How many of you know what it feels like to accomplish things and still not feel noticed? I remember getting an A on my report card and I was asked why I didn't get an A+? I will never forget that day because I knew that I would never be visible in the eyes of someone of whom I wanted approval. I decided that my accomplishments would be for me and the other people who noticed me.

I DID THE BEST I COULD

"WORDS FROM MY GRANDFATHER"

"I did the best I could". Until I turned 32, I used to despise that very sentence. I used to question within that if this was the best he could do, then why did he take on the responsibility of being a parent to my sisters and I? I did not understand what he meant when he said, "I did the best I could." I was just bitter and angry knowing I needed more from my grandfather and I felt he could've done better. I needed more encouragement and conversations. I needed to feel safe and loved. I needed to be open and fearless with him. Knowing all of my needs weren't met, I had to accept the toughest answer he would give "I did the best I could".

As I reflect back on my growing relationship with Christ, seeking therapy, and talking to other family members about grandpa's life, I realized this was all he could offer me at the time. I learned way more about his childhood and his adulthood life from the way he would think about women, addiction, and generational barriers that stopped him from being a better man. It helped me realize that he really did the best he could. What he gave me as a parent is what he was taught to offer. He didn't have what I needed, because it wasn't given to him in the way he needed. Therapy helped me learn how to voice my needs and give myself time to grieve. I can truly say those words "I did the best I could" has a totally different meaning now. Those words have helped me empathize with my grandpa and not judge him for what he didn't have to give.

THE INVISIBLE CHILD

A Poem

Dedicated to my deceased grandfather

Can you see me now? Can you see me now that you are in heaven? Are you looking down on me wishing things were different? Can you see the person that I've become? Can you see the woman that I've always wanted you to say you're proud of?

I was invisible to you all my life and I wonder if you can see the light shining on me now. I wonder if you can see the pain I carried watching you treat me like an outcast.

I wonder if you can see all the pain I buried, just so I could be visible.

I wonder if you can see me from heaven.

I wonder if you can see what I needed.

Can you see me now that you're not here anymore?

Can you see what you missed out on?

Can you see the growth in me?

Can you see the person screaming in silence

"I need my Daddy"?

Can you see the little girl reaching her hand out to you, but was ignored?

Can you see the little girl inside who still looks for you?

Can you see how I never felt protected?

Can you see the tears flowing down my face? Can you see me now offering grace?

Can you see what you've instilled in me? Can you see how sometimes I still want you to be there? Can you see the attention I needed?

Can you see what God has done... turned my pain around so the victory is won?

SECTION 4

EMOTIONAL ROLLERCOASTER

ABANDONMENT

REJECTION

ANGER

LIGHT SKIN SISTER VS. DARK SKIN SISTER

FATHERLESS DATING

19

ABANDONMENT

I felt abandoned for the majority of my life. Seeing my friends with their biological parents brought up so many emotions for me. Not being able to have the relationship with my father or even my grandfather was tough. I used to wonder, was it something I was doing wrong? What do I need to change in order to feel accepted and loved by my grandfather. I felt rejected as if I had no worth. All my heart desired was to belong. Instead, I felt like I was left alone.

"Even if my father and mother abandon me, the Lord will hold me close."

- Psalm 27:10 NLT

GOD'S RESPONSE TO ABANDONMENT

Once I surrendered to God, I could hear the Holy Spirit loud and clear. I remember sitting in my therapist's office in a ball of tears holding a teddy bear because I was sharing what I needed from my father. Once I got home and prayed, God brought me to a scripture that changed my life: Psalm 27:10 *Even if my father and mother abandon me, the Lord will hold me close.* This is the same scripture that helps me process my emotions daily.

It's okay to acknowledge your emotions. In this section, describe the emotion you are feeling regarding the relationship with your father?

NOTES

_____

_____

_____

_____

_____

_____

_____

_____

_____

_____

The Lord will hold me close.

- Psalm 27:10 NLT

REJECTION

I never felt accepted by my grandpa. I always felt rejected. Watching him show love in a different way towards two of my other siblings made me feel emotional. I used to think my grandpa was just showing tough love towards my siblings and I. I also used to think he just wanted structure. As time passed, I realized he *did* know how to show affection; just not to me. I struggled with rejection for years. That rejection also led me to become competitive with all of my friends and some family members. I wanted that feeling of acceptance so bad. It's one thing to think the parent who raised you didn't have the capacity to love the way you needed, but its another thing to watch him do it with one of my siblings.

For the Lord will not reject his people; he will never forsake his inheritance.

- Psalm 94:14 NLT

GOD'S RESPONSE TO REJECTION

I heard the Holy Spirit loud and clear: I chose you; so, you were never rejected
How can you be rejected when you are the daughter of the almighty king?

NOTES

_____

_____

_____

_____

_____

_____

_____

_____

_____

_____

For the Lord will not reject his people.

- Psalm 94:14 NLT

ANGER

I internalized so much anger towards my grandpa, especially as an adult. Every time I would have flashbacks about my childhood, I would always see my grandfather in a negative light. I realized I was still angry and I needed to release the anger in order to move forward.

Tapping into the anger emotion brought up feelings of hurt and a broken heart. I was angry because I wanted to be daddy's little girl. I was angry because I never got to have a dad & daughter date. I was angry because when I told my grandfather I was molested, he didn't believe me. It took hearing it from my little sister's mouth for him to believe it was true.

That was heartbreaking. I felt like my voice wasn't good enough for him.

In my adult years, the anger grew bigger and bigger as I ran away from my emotions. The feeling of anger pushed me to my healing place. In 2018, my grandfather passed away. I was surprisingly devastated. I loved my grandpa, but I didn't realize how angry I was with him until he passed away. Now that I have changed my perspective about my emotions, I know the anger had to take place in order to get to a healthy healing place.

Be angry, and do not sin.

- Ephesians 4:26 NKJV

GOD'S RESPONSE TO ANGER

It's okay to be angry and embrace your feelings, but do not act off of anger. "Deal with it", instead of ignoring it. Call on me and I will help you process it.

NOTES

_____
_____
_____
_____
_____
_____
_____
_____
_____
_____

Be angry, and do not sin.

- Ephesians 4:26 NKJV

LIGHT SKIN
VS. DARK SKIN SISTER

If I was only the light skin sister, I wonder what life would be like. Those were the thoughts I repeatedly played in my head over and over again. Growing up in a house with two light skin sisters and one dark skin sister was very weird to me. The dark skin sisters were treated differently than the light skin sisters.

At first, I used to think this was only in my head, but as I began to observe my grandpa, I realized it was because I was dark skin. I remember witnessing rules being thrown out the window for my light skin sisters, but with the dark skin sisters, all rules applied. I remember asking myself what is wrong with me? Do I need to bleach my skin to be loved? Do I need to run away so he could appreciate me? Do I stay the same and pray that you accept me for who I am?

That season of my life was rough. It's one thing for your parents to show a little favoritism to a sibling, but it's another when the favoritism is in your face and very obvious. The light skin sisters could date, the dark skin sisters couldn't. The light skin sisters didn't get punished for their wrong behavior, the dark skin sisters were overly punished. I remember asking my God-mom why my grandpa treated me this way? She did the best she could to help me with a great response, but she saw what went on in our household as well. She said that my grandpa was hard on me because he sees so much more in me. That response worked for the moment; but, it didn't work for long.

Being compared to my light skin sisters growing up affected my relationships with my light skin friends throughout my entire life. Not knowing that when I became friends with light skin women and even teenagers in high school, I'll begin to immediately compare myself to them and become jealous of them because of their skin tone. Their skin tone reminded me of how I was treated in the house where I grew up. Being around light skin teenagers and women made me feel like I wasn't good enough because that's what I saw in my household. I didn't realize this was happening until I begin my healing process as an adult doing therapy and through my relationship with Christ.

I used to wonder why I would feel inferior to my light skin friends as they were good friends to me. However, I was just confused about why I couldn't see them as true friends. I was confused that although they were good friends, I was still mad at them. Although they treated me kindly, I would still back away from them. Although they trusted me, I did not trust them. As I became an adult and discussed in therapy, it was revealed that I was still holding in anger from my childhood about being compared to my light skin sisters. I did not realize that all those years of comparison in my household with my grandpa affected my relationships as a woman and as a teenager. I did not know that how my grandpa treated my sisters and I would affect how I viewed my own skin for years. Today, I can truly say through healing and my love for Christ, I no longer feel inferior to my light skin sisters.

FATHERLESS DATING

Trying to date without a positive male role model in my household was very hard. I remember thinking I knew what it took to date because I witnessed other men in my family show love and support as husbands and fathers. Little did I know, the father figure that impacted my dating the most was my grandpa. Once I started dating in high school, I realized I was looking for that father figure's love and not a boyfriend. I was easily controlled and manipulated through college because I thought that was the norm. As I reflect on my college relationship, I remember thinking who taught me that being in this toxic relationship was okay. I stayed because I felt a sense of protection and love, but in reality it was fear of being alone. The guy was older than me; so, I felt like he acted like my father. Sounds weird, but my heart was attracted to a father figure and not to a mate.

Experiencing toxic relationships, I realized I was never taught how to have standards as a woman. I didn't have high expectations for men. Whatever they said, I would usually go with it. I needed a father figure to sit me down and have a conversation about standards. All I saw growing up in my household was my grandma dealing with verbally abusive language and she still served my grandfather. Witnessing those dynamics, I thought I was supposed to allow men to treat me however they wanted and I was supposed to stand by them. My standards were chosen by my father figure's character.

SECTION 5

FATHERLESS
AFFIRMATIONS

8-DAYS OF JOURNAL
PROMPTS

DADDY/DAUGHTER DANCE

SOCIETY CHART

STEPS TO NURTURE
INNER CHILD

FATHERLESS AFFIRMATION

I am worthy even in your absence.
Your absence has a purpose for my
life.
I am not a mistake.
I am healing every area that was
broken.
Your absence will not dictate my
relationships.
I will surround myself with healthy
individuals during my healing process.
The relationship between my parents
will not dictate my future
relationships.
Forgiving my father is for me, not for
him.
I will not allow my past burdens to
keep me from my future blessings.
I am Loved.
I am Called.
My experiences are valid.
My feelings are valid.
I am being used for God's Glory.
There is no storm or obstacle that
can take away my assignment
on this earth.
I am a Change Agent for the
fatherless.

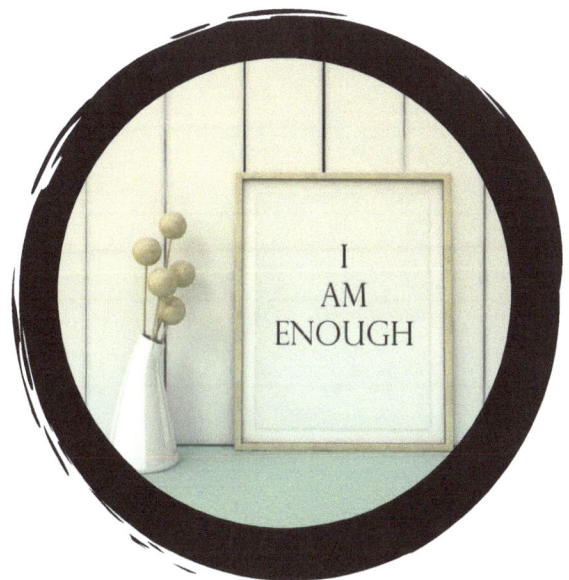

Day #1: Journal Prompts
Healing the Fatherless Heart

The number 8 represents new beginnings. As you begin this healing journal, there will be a newness as you release. In this section, you will journal eight days using these journal prompts. Writing is a form of healing. Remember to be honest with yourself!

Why Me? Why Not Me?

_____

_____

_____

_____

_____

_____

_____

_____

_____

_____

_____

_____

_____

Day #2: Journal Prompts
Healing the Fatherless Heart

Welcome to Day #2.
Today, you will focus on the word Forgiveness. Don't give up. Forgiveness allows you to let go and live. Remember: Vulnerability is normal.

Forgiving my father looks like...

_____

_____

_____

_____

_____

_____

_____

_____

_____

_____

_____

Day #3: Journal Prompts
Healing the Fatherless Heart

Welcome to Day #3.
Today, you will focus on celebrating you. Remember it's okay to celebrate yourself.

I am proud of myself for...

_____

_____

_____

_____

_____

_____

_____

_____

_____

_____

Day #4: Journal Prompts
Healing the Fatherless Heart

Welcome to Day #4.
Today, you will focus on how your life story helped you. Remember to focus on the positive things today.

The absence of my father helped me... _____

_____

_____

_____

_____

_____

_____

_____

_____

_____

_____

_____

Day #5: Journal Prompts
Healing the Fatherless Heart

Welcome to Day #5.
Today, is the day you will acknowledge your purpose. Remember: You were placed on this earth for a reason.

I am not a mistake.

_____

_____

_____

_____

_____

_____

_____

_____

_____

_____

_____

Day #6: Journal Prompts
Healing the Fatherless Heart

Welcome to Day #6.
Today, you will focus on understanding. Remember to focus on your perspective.

I understand now...

_____

_____

_____

_____

_____

_____

_____

_____

_____

_____

_____

Day #7: Journal Prompts
Healing the Fatherless Heart

Welcome to Day #7.
Today, you will focus on how your father's absence affects your relationships. Remember to release everything negative that you felt during these relationships.

The absence of my father affected my relationships by...

_____

_____

_____

_____

_____

_____

_____

_____

_____

_____

_____

Day #8: Journal Prompts
Healing the Fatherless Heart

Congrats! It's Day #8.
Today, you will affirm and discuss how daddy issues stop with you. Remember: You are setting the tone for future generations.

Daddy issues stop with me.

_____

_____

_____

_____

_____

_____

_____

_____

_____

_____

_____

DADDY/DAUGHTER DANCE

As I sit Indian style with my eyes closed, I can see my daddy and I at our first daddy/daughter dance. I have on a pink dress with ruffles, a crown on my head, and a little lipstick on my lips. I can see my dad with a black suit, Steve Madden black shoes, and a pink bow tie. Wow! My dad looks sharp! Next, I hear the DJ playing Daddy by Beyonce. I love this song. The DJ asks everyone to come to the dance floor with their dads. I am so excited to show off my dad. My dad grabs my hand, picks me up, and walks to the dance floor. Dancing with him feels safe.

Then, I opened my eyes and realize this was just my imagination. Maybe, one day I will get that chance to dance with my father.

Use your imagination and experience your father. Close your eyes. Visualize being with him at a dance, park, sports event or even at your home. On the page that follows, write down what you can see, touch, and hear. Write down any emotions that surfaced as you are completing this exercise.

NOTES

_____

_____

_____

_____

_____

_____

_____

_____

_____

_____

Use your imagination

40

- Laurie Ford

SOCIETY CHART

What society has trained you to say:	**Reframing your words to validate your feeling:**
Not having a father makes you more independent	My father's absence made me feel as though I couldn't depend on anyone
At least, I had a stepdad	Desiring a relationship with my biological father doesn't mean I don't value my relationship with my stepdad
Your mom was a single mom; so she was your mom and dad	I appreciate my mom for raising me, but I also needed my father's love

THE STEPS TO NURTURING THE FATHERLESS INNER CHILD

Step 1
Acknowledge your emotions

- Verbalize the emotions you're feeling
- Listen to what your inner child is saying
- Use a journal to release your emotions
- Write a letter from your adult prospective

Step 2
Speak to yourself with a Calm voice

- The inner child needs to hear a calm voice so he/she won't go in protective mode or shut down
- Try a form of meditation to be present with your feelings

Step 3
Reassure the inner child

- Reassure your inner child by letting him/her know they are safe
- Remind your inner child that what they are experiecing is a new situation

THE STEPS TO NURTURING THE FATHERLESS INNER CHILD

Step 4
Affirmations

- Speak Life to your inner child
- Create positive affirmations
- Read the affirmations daily
- Place the affirmations around your home

Step 5
Key Phrases

- I Love You
- I Hear You
- You didn't deserve this
- Thank You

SECTION 6

MY STORY MADE CLEAR BY GOD

DNA TEST

GOD IS THE FATHER TO THE FATHERLESS

SOLUTION TO MY DADDY ISSUES

HEAVENLY VS EARTHLY FATHER

INVISIBLE VS VISIBLE TO GOD

BLACK SHEEP

DNA TEST

As a 13 year old teenager, hearing the words, "I found your father", meant the world to me. I was so excited to finally meet my father. My sister and I shared the same excitement leading up to the day of the DNA test. I remember meeting him and exchanging numbers. I think I blew up his phone daily until the test results came back. As I sat patiently in the courtroom waiting for the judge to share the result, I was so nervous.

"What if he isn't my dad? What if he is? Ok, Laurie. Calm down."

The judge opened the paper and stated, "You are NOT the Father." My heart was broken. Wait, I look just like him! We are the same height! What happened? I was very disappointed. How could I be so stupid to believe it was actually my time to be happy? I remember going home so mad at my mom. She was staying with us at the time. She was in the kitchen cooking. I could tell she already knew what I was going to say, but I asked anyway. I asked why she would assure my sister and I that our father was found if he wasn't our dad. She replied honestly that she was not sure who my father was. She stated that she was intoxicated at the time I was conceived and can't remember who my father is. She said that she was sorry for not being honest. Although I was very hurt, I understood she couldn't tell me something she couldn't remember. From that day forward I didn't get my hope ups. It was hard, but I didn't want to feel disappointed again. I felt that this chapter of my life was closed because the only person who would know about my father had no knowledge of who he was.

GOD IS THE FATHER TO THE FATHERLESS

As I began to read the Bible and get to know God's character more, I realized God was the father I was searching for. I realized God is who I needed daily. Although I wanted my earthly father, I wasn't aware that my Heavenly Father could fill every void in my life. I grew up in church, but never experienced a true relationship with God. Once I rededicated my life to Christ in 2015, there was no turning back.

Reading my Bible made me feel like a queen. The way God saw me in His eyes was like no other. I remember thinking, "God, no one has ever talked to me with so much love and confidence." When I realized I was chosen, called, redeemed, loved, forgiven, His masterpiece, workmanship, and His royal daughter, there was no turning back for me. In God's presence, I found so much peace. Nothing matters in those moments. Bills don't matter, my bank account doesn't matter, or even family drama is out of the window in God's presence.

GOD IS THE FATHER I WAS SEARCHING FOR.

-LAURIE FORD

This was a feeling I never felt before. I gained that safety and protection I was looking for on earth. I gained the confidence I wanted from my earthly father. God showed me through His Word and presence that everything I needed was in Him.

46

THE SOLUTION TO MY DADDY ISSUES: A RELATIONSHIP WITH MY HEAVENLY FATHER!

How I saw God was through my relationship with my own father and grandfather! I didn't want anything to do with God because I knew if I had to look at the character of my earthly fathers, I would be disappointed in God as well. Through experience I thought that there is no compassion. Through my lens I was never good enough for my grandfather, so I struggled when God told me He chose me. I struggled with knowing I was loved and important to God, because growing up I never felt that way. I didn't feel visible to my grandfather so how could I be visible to God? I used to ask myself questions such as: When will I become visible to my grandfather? Does he even see me? Does he care about me? Does he realize how much I need his love and protection?

It took me years to accept God as my father. It wasn't easy to accept God when I compared Him to my unknown father and my grandfather. I know now that God isn't like anyone on earth. Once I realized He created me and knew my purpose before I was even born, helped me to see God from a different lens. I later began to trust God as my father and surrendered to His plans for my life. That was one of the hardest and most joyous moment in my life!

No longer being in control of my life was hard, although I realized when I was in control I was lacking everything.

Once I built a relationship with God and started to see his character I was convinced that I was loved, chosen, and never abandoned!

> GOD IS MY FATHER AND I SURRENDERED TO HIS PLAN FOR MY LIFE.
>
> -LAURIE FORD

HEAVENLY
VS. EARTHLY FATHER

HEAVENLY FATHER

- Father that will not disappoint you
- Father that will never leave you
- Father who protects and cover you
- Father who won't abandon you
- Father who loves unconditionally
- Perfect Father

VS

EARTHLY FATHER

- Father is human and may disappoint you
- Father who makes mistakes
- Father whose love can wane
- Father who will make poor choices
- Father who struggles with the earthly mindset

INVISIBLE VS. VISIBLE TO GOD

I remember like it was yesterday... feeling invisible. So many emotions arose as I watched my siblings receive the attention I desired from my grandfather. I grew up in a house full of women and I wasn't seen. I felt the pain of feeling unheard. I was overcome with the sting of not being able to use my voice. It felt horrible to not be able to advocate or speak up for myself. Imagine this bold child with so much energy and so much purpose, but had to dim her light around the person who should have been a force of encouragement for her. This person she called her grandfather. What if he had enhanced my purpose allowing me to speak up and flourish in the gifts God has given me?

However, he suffered with insecurities; so, how could he help me with mine? He suffered with addiction; so, his judgment was clouded to seeing me. He couldn't see me. But I didn't let this be an excuse. I acknowledged his insufficiencies and refused to give in. God showed me how to move forward in my gifts in spite of the time that was lost. He showed me how to move forward from the tears I cried and from those days of feeling invisible. I know now that God is my father; I am visible to him. I am more visible to myself and others and I am finally able to speak my mind and to love and advocate for myself, set boundaries, and become the best version of who God created me to be. My voice is no longer silent. Now, when I walk into any room, people see my presence instead of my pain. And when I leave the room, people see a bold legacy instead of fear and anxiety. Knowing I'm visible to God, my Heavenly Father, gives me that irreplaceable confidence and joy.

THE BLACK SHEEP OF THE FAMILY

Hearing the term the black sheep didn't sit well with me for years. Knowing that I was different and I was set apart from individuals in my family sometimes made me insecure and feel inferior to others around me. Once I got a relationship with God, He showed me that being the black sheep was a part of my purpose. God showed me that if I wasn't the black sheep, I would have conformed to everyone else. I wouldn't know how to operate in the gifts He'd already put inside me.

When I heard the words "black sheep", I heard darkness, discrimination, and pain. But now that I've healed, those words no longer hold me back from what God has for me. When I hear "the black sheep", I hear boldness and that I was created to stand out. Though I must admit, being the black sheep as a grown-up isn't all gravy today. As I stand out and I stand for what God has for me, I realize the Black sheep had to be used as a part of my purpose. I didn't feel good going to family functions feeling like I wasn't enough and that I didn't fit in. I chose to think, act and talk differently from the family norm. I chose to not hide myself and to put myself and my education first. I chose to live a life that would be full of purpose and legacy, different from how I was always known... the black sheep. It wasn't easy at all and I didn't feel confident all the time until I reached my mid-20s. I realized that being a black sheep meant sacrificing and being ok with being and thinking differently.

Being the black sheep often meant that I had to be the only one who advocated and stood up for what was morally right. I had to be OK with that whether it was standing up against family or not. I used to think how could I be in this family and think so different from everyone else. Then I had to realize that God chose me to be that living example. Even unacknowledged, I know that God has called me to a higher standard to be set apart to do His Will. So, I surrendered to His Will and Way as a chosen vessel to be an example in my family.

BLACK SHEEP VS. GOD'S SHEEP

BLACK SHEEP

- Treated different by family or friends
- Teased for being different
- Judged for having different ideas or conversations
- Often called arrogant or bougie
- The odd ball
- Less valuable
- Top of the family discussions

VS

GOD'S SHEEP

- Stands out
- Accepts being different
- Masterpiece
- Focus on the truth even if it means not agreeing with the majority
- Royalty
- Operates and makes decisions by the Spirit
- Understands God's plans are bigger than your own
- Knows that everything good and bad works out for the good of those who loves Christ
- Created to be bold
- Understands the importance of faith, love, and obedience

SECTION 7

ORDAINED WORTHY

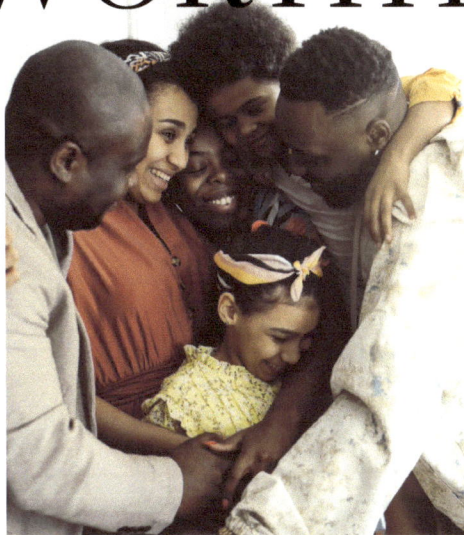

I used to struggle with feeling worthy, because I didn't know my identity. I used to wonder how can God use me when I don't even know where I came from. My father is unknown and my mother can't raise me. "WHO AM I, God?" I thought I was a mistake. I thought my life had no purpose. I struggled with feeling rejected and abandoned. "Why am I here, God?" Those are the questions that crossed my mind daily. "Why would you place me on earth without my mother and father?" As I began the healing process, God showed me exactly why I was placed on earth. He showed me how every detail of my story will be used for His Glory. He showed me how to turn all of my scars into His beauty marks. He told me that I was His chosen child.

One day, while watching Bible study on Facebook Live, I heard the Holy Spirit loud and clear say, "I ordained you worthy when your mom was lying on the abortion table and the doctors told her she was a week too late and she couldn't abort you." Those words literally took my breath away. Hearing the Holy Spirit say "I ordained you worthy in the womb" was life changing. Hearing those words brought so much clarity to my life. He showed me that no matter what my life looks like, I am supposed to be on this earth.

Releasing the Guilt

Sometimes, we hold on to guilt because it makes us feel comfortable and allows us to run away from our feelings instead of embracing them. When I think about the things that I went through as a child growing up under my grandpa's leadership, I can't help but think of generational curses. Everything that my grandpa did not do for me or could not provide for me, I've realized it wasn't provided for him. It took me forever to get to this mindset, but by the grace of God and seeking God's face, He allowed me to see that it's not my fault. It's not my fault that I was treated differently. It's not my fault that I grew up in an angry household. It's not my fault that I was born into generational alcoholism. Once the Lord showed me that my grandpa was mentally or physically unable to give me what he didn't have, I remember feeling a sense of peace. After talking with different family members, I realized he did not have the best upbringing. I started to feel more compassion for his mindset. Having compassion allowed me to release the guilt that I was holding on to knowing that as a release I am being set free.

A FATHER'S TOUCH

I desired a fathers touch to give me a feeling of safety and protection. A feeling that only a father knows how to give. I remember as a child the desire to just hear the words 'I love you' from my grandfather. What would it feel like to get off of the school bus, run into the house, and jump in my grandfather's arms with excitement to see him? I remember imagining this scenario in my head.

Draw a picture of what you desired from your father that you didn't get. Ex: A picture of your father helping you tie your shoe. Remember this picture doesn't have to be perfect. This is healing in your work of art.

Fatherless HEALING PROCESS

Healing doesn't always look pretty. Sitting in your feelings does not feel good at times. Knowing that you may never know your father's name is not appealing at all. As I write my story, I had to become more vulnerable. As I fought through tears during the healing process, the Holy Spirit spoke to me and stated there is healing and deliverance when you are vulnerable. It's hard being vulnerable when you are running from the emotions. However, after a lot of prayer, crying and fasting, I realized my vulnerability brings healing to me and other people. I worked through my healing by seeking God's presence and going to therapy.

Taking steps towards your healing journey may not be easy, but it is worth it. Things to remember as you are going on this journey:

1. Acknowledge your current emotions
2. Spend time with your higher power
3. Seek a professional therapist who can help you with your process with no judgment
4. Journal about your true feelings
5. Spend time alone to visualize the outcome you desire after healing
6. Talk to a friend or a family member you can trust when you need encouragement
7. Remember the healing process takes time
8. Don't compare your healing process to everyone else's
9. Create positive affirmations and post them where you can see them as reminders on those tough days
10. Incorporate exercise during your healing process

LETTER FROM YOUR HEAVENLY FATHER

Dear _____,

You are not alone. When you lay down and you feel empty, I am with you. When you are looking for an earthly father figure, I will send you someone who will love you like I do. When you have no words to say because you are hurting, I am still with you. I will give you the words to say. I will place the right people around you to love you like I do. I will comfort you when you need it most. I am your Heavenly Father, and I love you. When you have days that you don't want to look in the mirror, remember everything I create is a masterpiece. When you are searching for a mate, remember my love is unconditional. When you are trying to put it all together in your head and it's not making sense, remember you can cast your cares and worries on me because I care for you. I am your Heavenly Father, and I will make all things new!

Love,

Your Heavenly Father

MY HAPPY ENDING

I was told by many people that I lived in a fantasy world. I never understood what that meant until now. As a child I used my imagination often because there was no disappointment in my head. Wherever I wanted to go and whatever I want to do, I could if I used my imagination. Waiting for a happy ending to my life's story created layers of anger. I became angry because that happy ending I made up in my head wasn't my reality. I didn't want to share my story until it sounded happy. I remember being angry because I didn't want to share my feelings with others about my father until I met my biological father. Coming to terms with the fact that my happy ending won't look like my imagination was tough. However, through the healing process my happy ending was establishing a solid relationship and foundation in Christ. My happy ending is my healing place. My happy ending is breaking the cycle of bringing children into this world without a father. My happy ending is not what I expected, but it's what was chosen for me. My happy ending is knowing my story is still being written.

In this section describe your happy ending. What does this look like? How do you feel? What do you see?

NOTES

_____

_____

_____

_____

_____

_____

_____

_____

_____

_____

My happy ending is still being written.

— Laurie Ford

CONGRATS!

You've stepped out of your comfort zone and faced your emotions. There is nothing or no one holding you back from what is yours.

You did it! Celebrate this win! There is power when you speak your truth.

I am proud of you!

Love,
Laurie Ford
Fatherless Change Agent

MORE FROM THE AUTHOR

BOOKS & MERCHANDISE

- You Are Enough: *How to Heal From Your Couch Therapy Workbook*
- I Am Enough: *Affirmation Journal*
- Generational Curse Breaker Tees & Tops
- I Am Enough Tees & Tops

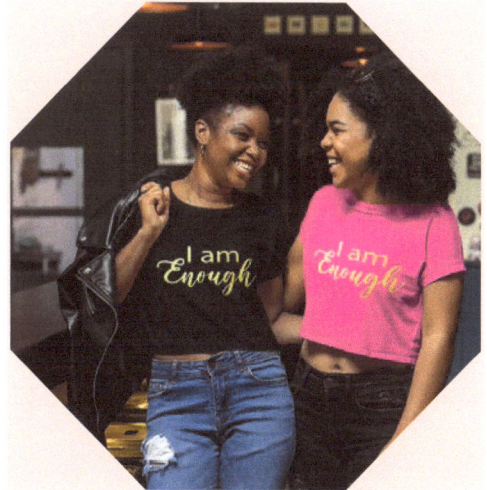

COUNSELING SERVICES

- Individual Therapy
- Group Therapy
- Online Therapy
- Consultations
- Master Classes
- Speaking Engagements

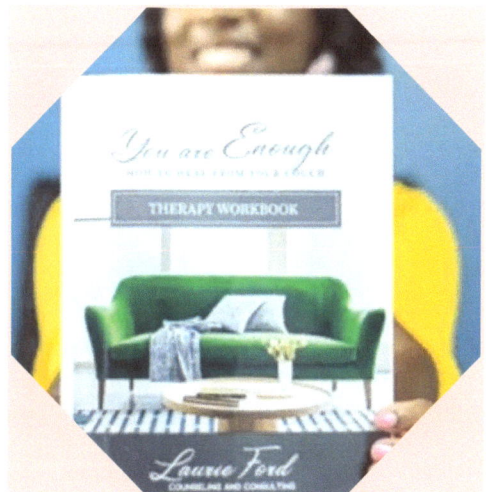

CONTACT

Website:
lfordcounseling.com

Facebook:
l.fordcounseling

Instagram:
_mrs.fordcounseling

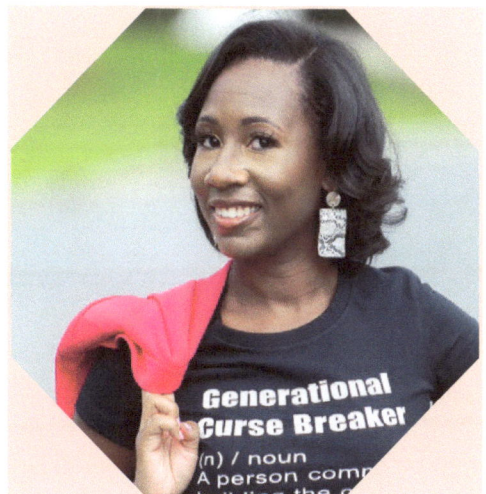

www.ingramcontent.com/pod-product-compliance
Lightning Source LLC
Chambersburg PA
CBHW060859270326
41935CB00003B/29